THE ANTS GO MARCHING

Retold by NICHOLAS IAN

Illustrations by TIM PALIN

Music by MARK OBLINGER

CANTATA LEARNING

WWW.CANTATALEARNING.COM

CANTATA
LEARNING

Published by Cantata Learning
1710 Roe Crest Drive
North Mankato, MN 56003
www.cantatalearning.com

A note to educators and librarians from the publisher: Cantata Learning has provided the following data to assist in book processing and suggested use of Cantata Learning product.

Publisher's Cataloging-in-Publication Data
Prepared by Librarian Consultant: Ann-Marie Begnaud
Library of Congress Control Number: 2016938098
    The Ants Go Marching
    Series: Sing-along Songs : Math
    Retold by Nicholas Ian
    Illustrations by Tim Palin
    Music by Mark Oblinger
    Summary: Counting by twos is made easy in this twist on the classic song The Ants Go Marching.
    ISBN: 978-1-63290-800-1 (library binding/CD)
Suggested Dewey and Subject Headings:
    Dewey: E 513.21
    LCSH Subject Headings: Mathematics – Juvenile literature. | Mathematics – Songs and music – Texts. | Mathematics –
Juvenile sound recordings.
    Sears Subject Headings: Counting. | Addition. | School songbooks. | Children's songs. | Jazz music.
    BISAC Subject Headings: JUVENILE NONFICTION / Concepts / Counting & Numbers. | JUVENILE NONFICTION /
Music / Songbooks. | JUVENILE NONFICTION / Mathematics / Arithmetic.

Book design and art direction: Tim Palin Creative
Editorial direction: Flat Sole Studio
Music direction: Elizabeth Draper
Music written and produced by Mark Oblinger

Printed in the United States of America in North Mankato, Minnesota.
122016   0339CGS17

ACCESS THE MUSIC!

SCAN CODE WITH MOBILE APP

CANTATALEARNING.COM

TIPS TO SUPPORT LITERACY AT HOME

WHY READING AND SINGING WITH YOUR CHILD IS SO IMPORTANT

Daily reading with your child leads to increased academic achievement. Music and songs, specifically rhyming songs, are a fun and easy way to build early literacy and language development. Music skills correlate significantly with both phonological awareness and reading development. Singing helps build vocabulary and speech development. And reading and appreciating music together is a wonderful way to strengthen your relationship.

READ AND SING EVERY DAY!

TIPS FOR USING CANTATA LEARNING BOOKS AND SONGS DURING YOUR DAILY STORY TIME

1. As you sing and read, point out the different words on the page that rhyme. Suggest other words that rhyme.

2. Memorize simple rhymes such as Itsy Bitsy Spider and sing them together. This encourages comprehension skills and early literacy skills.

3. Use the questions in the back of each book to guide your singing and storytelling.

4. Read the included sheet music with your child while you listen to the song. How do the music notes correlate to the words of the song?

5. Sing along on the go and at home. Access music by scanning the QR code on each Cantata book, or by using the included CD. You can also stream or download the music for free to your computer, smartphone, or mobile device.

Devoting time to daily reading shows that you are available for your child. Together, you are building language, literacy, and listening skills.

Have fun reading and singing!

In this song, where there's one ant, there are two! The ants travel in pairs. As the ants march along, more ants join them, two at a time.

Turn the page and count by twos as the ants try to get out of the rain. Remember to sing and march along!

The ants go marching two by two. **Hurrah**! Hurrah!
The ants go marching two by two. Hurrah! Hurrah!

The ants go marching two by two.
The little one stops to tie his shoe,
and they all go marching down to the ground
to get out of the rain. Boom! Boom! Boom!

The ants go marching four by four. Hurrah! Hurrah!
The ants go marching four by four. Hurrah! Hurrah!

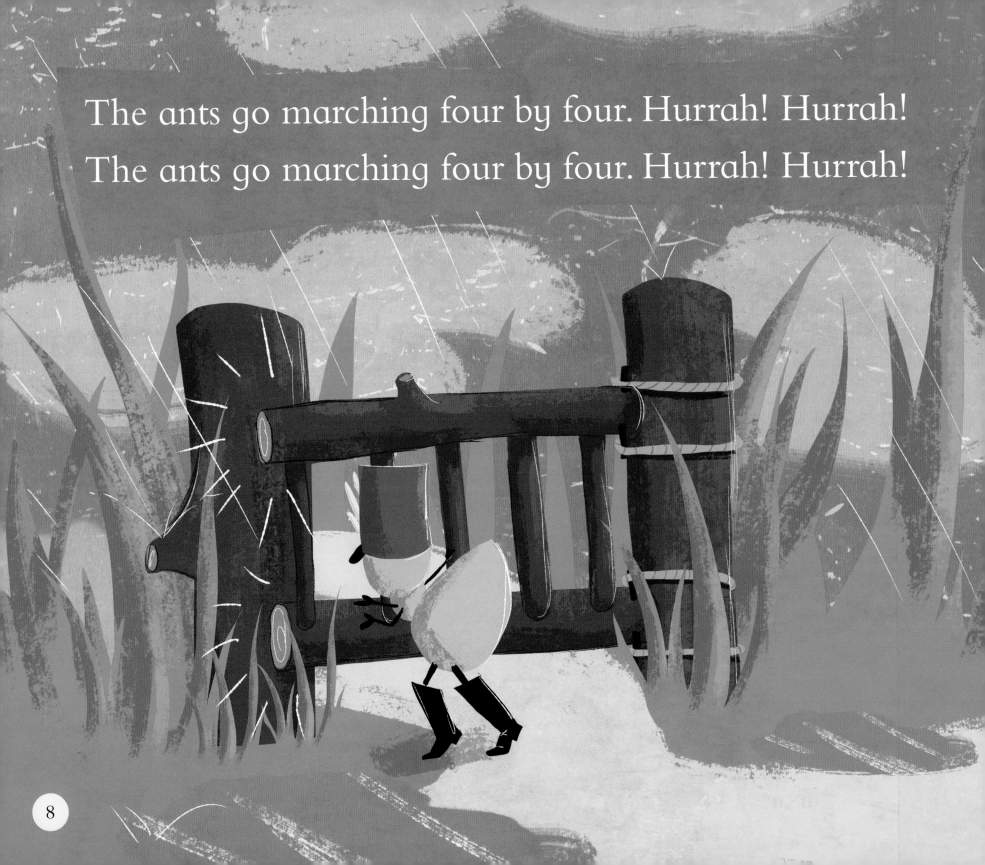

The ants go marching four by four.
The little one stops to shut the door,
and they all go marching down to the ground
to get out of the rain. Boom! Boom! Boom!

The ants go marching six by six. Hurrah! Hurrah!
The ants go marching six by six. Hurrah! Hurrah!

The ants go marching six by six.
The little one stops to pick up sticks,
and they all go marching down to the ground
to get out of the rain. Boom! Boom! Boom!

The ants go marching eight by eight. Hurrah! Hurrah!
The ants go marching eight by eight. Hurrah! Hurrah!

The ants go marching eight by eight.
The little one stops to shut the gate,
and they all go marching down to the ground
to get out of the rain. Boom! Boom! Boom!

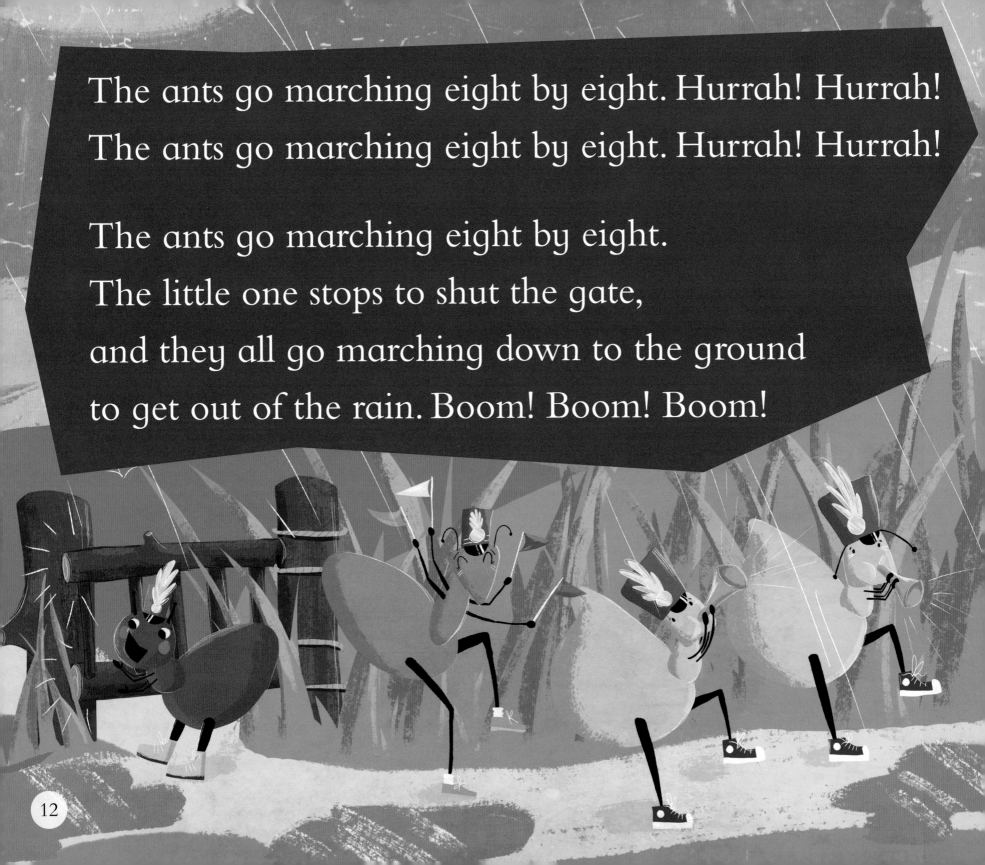

The ants go marching ten by ten. Hurrah! Hurrah!
The ants go marching ten by ten. Hurrah! Hurrah!

The ants go marching ten by ten.
The little one shouts, "Do it again!"

And they all go marching down to the ground to get out of the rain. Boom! Boom! Boom!

15

The ants go marching with their friends—
two, four, six, eight, and ten!
You and your pal stomp around.
Stomp around upon the ground.

Boom! Boom! Boom! Boom! Boom!

17

Let's march and stomp around the room.
Hurrah! Hurrah!

18

Let's march and stomp around the room.
Hurrah! Hurrah!

The ants go marching with their friends—
two, four, six, eight, and ten!
You and your pal stomp around.
Stomp around upon the ground.

Boom! Boom! Boom! Boom! Boom!

SONG LYRICS
The Ants Go Marching

The ants go marching two by two. Hurrah! Hurrah!
The ants go marching two by two. Hurrah! Hurrah!

The ants go marching two by two.
The little one stops to tie his shoe,
and they all go marching down to the ground
to get out of the rain. Boom! Boom! Boom!

The ants go marching four by four. Hurrah! Hurrah!
The ants go marching four by four. Hurrah! Hurrah!

The ants go marching four by four.
The little one stops to shut the door,
and they all go marching down to the ground
to get out of the rain. Boom! Boom! Boom!

The ants go marching six by six. Hurrah! Hurrah!
The ants go marching six by six. Hurrah! Hurrah!

The ants go marching six by six.
The little one stops to pick up sticks,
and they all go marching down to the ground
to get out of the rain. Boom! Boom! Boom!

The ants go marching eight by eight. Hurrah! Hurrah!
The ants go marching eight by eight. Hurrah! Hurrah!

The ants go marching eight by eight.
The little one stops to shut the gate,
and they all go marching down to the ground
to get out of the rain. Boom! Boom! Boom!

The ants go marching ten by ten. Hurrah! Hurrah!
The ants go marching ten by ten. Hurrah! Hurrah!

The ants go marching ten by ten.
The little one shouts, "Do it again!"
And they all go marching down to the ground
to get out of the rain. Boom! Boom! Boom!

Let's march and stomp around the room. Hurrah! Hurrah!
Let's march and stomp around the room. Hurrah! Hurrah!

The ants go marching with their friends—two, four, six,
    eight, and ten!
You and your pal stomp around. Stomp around upon
    the ground.
Boom! Boom! Boom! Boom! Boom!

Let's march and stomp around the room. Hurrah! Hurrah!
Let's march and stomp around the room. Hurrah! Hurrah!

The ants go marching with their friends—two, four, six,
    eight, and ten!
You and your pal stomp around. Stomp around upon
    the ground.
Boom! Boom! Boom! Boom! Boom!

The Ants Go Marching

Jazz
Mark Oblinger

Verses 1–5

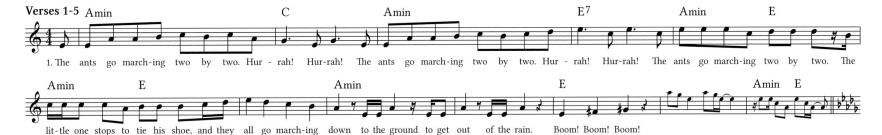

1. The ants go march-ing two by two. Hur-rah! Hur-rah! The ants go march-ing two by two. Hur-rah! Hur-rah! The ants go march-ing two by two. The lit-tle one stops to tie his shoe, and they all go march-ing down to the ground to get out of the rain. Boom! Boom! Boom!

Verse 2
The ants go marching four by four. Hurrah! Hurrah!
The ants go marching four by four. Hurrah! Hurrah!
The ants go marching four by four.
The little one stops to shut the door,
and they all go marching down to the ground
to get out of the rain. Boom! Boom! Boom!

Verse 3
The ants go marching six by six. Hurrah! Hurrah!
The ants go marching six by six. Hurrah! Hurrah!
The ants go marching six by six.
The little one stops to pick up sticks,
and they all go marching down to the ground
to get out of the rain. Boom! Boom! Boom!

Verse 4
The ants go marching eight by eight. Hurrah! Hurrah!
The ants go marching eight by eight. Hurrah! Hurrah!
The ants go marching eight by eight.
The little one stops to shut the gate,
and they all go marching down to the ground
to get out of the rain. Boom! Boom! Boom!

Verse 5
The ants go marching ten by ten. Hurrah! Hurrah!
The ants go marching ten by ten. Hurrah! Hurrah!
The ants go marching ten by ten.
The little one shouts, "Do it again!"
And they all go marching down to the ground
to get out of the rain. Boom! Boom! Boom!

Verses 6–7

6. Let's march and stomp a-round the room. Hur-rah! Hur-rah! Let's march and stomp a-round the room. Hur-rah! Hur-rah! The ants go march-ing with their friends— two, four, six, eight, and ten! You and your pal stomp a-round. Stomp a-round up-on the ground. Boom! Boom! Boom! Boom! Boom!

(Instrumental Interlude)

Verse 7
Let's march and stomp around the room. Hurrah! Hurrah!
Let's march and stomp around the room. Hurrah! Hurrah!
The ants go marching with their friends—two, four, six, eight, and ten!
You and your pal stomp around. Stomp around upon the ground.
Boom! Boom! Boom! Boom! Boom!

GLOSSARY

hurrah—a cheer of excitement

stomp—to walk with very heavy steps

GUIDED READING ACTIVITIES

1. Look around you. Can you find two of anything? How about four of something? Six? Eight? Ten? List the things you found.

2. Practice counting by twos with pennies. Start with two pennies. Then add two more so that you have four. Keep adding two pennies to see how high you can count.

3. With a black or brown marker or crayon, draw two ants. Can you draw them marching?

TO LEARN MORE

Adamson, Thomas K., and Heather Adamson. *2, 4, Skip Count Some More*. North Mankato, MN: Capstone, 2012.

Rissman, Rebecca. *Counting at the Park*. North Mankato, MN: Heinemann-Raintree, 2013.

Steffora, Tracey. *Adding with Ants*. North Mankato, MN: Heinemann-Raintree, 2014.

Steffora, Tracey. *Skip Counting with Meerkats*. North Mankato, MN: Heinemann-Raintree, 2014.